Ian Falkner is a member of the Ramblers' Association. He's been leading a local rambling group in Kent for over 28 years. As a member of the local historical society, he has developed a keen interest in those parts of Kent, Surrey and Sussex where he has walked... and would like to pass on such information that he has gleaned from his research to a wider audience.

To the Edenbridge Strollers, whose idea it was that I should write this book.

Ian Falkner

STROLLING THROUGH THREE COUNTIES

AUSTIN MACAULEY PUBLISHERS™

LONDON • CAMBRIDGE • NEW YORK • SHARJAH

A CIP catalogue record for this title is available from the British Library.

ISBN 9781788481465 (Paperback)
ISBN 9781788481472 (Hardback)
ISBN 9781528954204 (ePub e-book)

www.austinmacauley.com

First Published (2019)
Austin Macauley Publishers Ltd
25 Canada Square
Canary Wharf
London
E14 5LQ

To David and Janet, without whose help this book would not have been written.

Contents

Introduction

Twenty-five years ago, three people and a dog went on a short walk around the countryside of Edenbridge.

After 25 years, that group has expanded into a full-blown rambling group. Also the group has expanded its horizons to stretch into the depths of Kent, Surrey and Sussex.

So we thought this might be an opportune time to share with you some of the delightful walks we have been on; also, and just as important, to point out some of the interesting landmarks and stunning viewpoints that we came across.

In some cases, I have been able to specify the serial numbers of footpaths and bridleways on the routes. These can be useful navigational tools: FP = footpath; BW = bridleway.

A word of warning: the countryside is not set in stone. Footpaths sometimes get diverted, hedges grubbed out or replaced, arable fields turned into grazing fields or vice versa. It has even been known for authors to make mistakes. So if you find an error in the text, don't grumble to your mate in the pub about it. Write to me c/o the publisher so that any errors can be corrected in any future reprint.

1. Through a Birdcage

Circular Walk from Chiddingstone Causeway (Penshurst Station)

(6 miles)

OS Explorer Map 147

Grid REF: TQ 520 158

1. This walk is easily accessible by bus (hourly service between Tunbridge Wells and Edenbridge on weekdays) and train (hourly service between Redhill & Tonbridge) as well as by car.

2. We parked our cars in the Station Approach Road; this needs to be done with caution in view of the large lorries using the adjacent timber yard.

Leigh village green

3. From the car park, we crossed the footbridge at Penshurst Station (rather confusingly named since it is located two miles from Penshurst Village) out of the

station and up the short Approach Road to the B2027 Tonbridge Rd. We crossed this road to the Little Brown Jug Public House (a rather more salubrious establishment than what at one time was a random public house, where the local livestock wandered at will among the customers in the bar and garden).

4. We followed the road right past St Luke's Church (designed by the same architect who designed Westminster RC Cathedral) and opposite the B2176 Road to Penshurst Village. We took a tarmac path (FP416) on the left which leads to the hamlet of Charcott. The field on the right has previously been used as a private airfield and a polo pitch. During the Second World War, it was requisitioned as an emergency airfield.

5. The tarmac path comes out at a minor road (Coppins Rd) without pavement or grass verge, where we turned right and then left (D282) to Charcott. We passed the Greyhound Public House on our right, and followed the road into the driveway of Charcott Farm (FP403).

6. Soon after entering this driveway and before reaching the farmhouse, we crossed a stile on our right where the original path had been diverted and crossed diagonally across a grazing field, taking the left of the two field paths to a gate at a junction of paths (left, straight ahead and right). We took the right-hand path adjacent to the headland, eventually crossing a footbridge over a ditch stream and emerging into an open field where we crossed diagonally left to the driveway of Wickhurst Farm. We then walked past the farmhouse till the driveway emerged at Coppins Road. Opposite, we crossed a footbridge over a ditch stream and followed the path left at the side of the hedge (FP411) to the farm road where we turned right to Leigh Park Farm (FP410). We crossed a stile into a field on the right and followed the path through a second field into a wood. This section of the path is known as birdcage walk – the remains of the curved iron railings perhaps provide a clue to the derivation of this name. Through the trees on the right, it is possible to see the lake of

Hall Place and the house itself. The gardens are open annually in May, under the National Gardens Scheme. The walk around the lake, with its surrounding azaleas and wisterias, is worth seeing. The house itself is badly in need of repair, but apparently, neither the owner nor the local authority are in a position to carry out the work. At one time, the Elizabethan red-brick house was occupied by Samuel Morley, the 19th century Nottingham merchant and local philanthropist, who was responsible for the building of several cottages in the main road running through the village of Leigh (sometimes spelt as *Lyghe* which is why it is pronounced as *Lie*). The footpath emerges at the end of the wood into a grazing field, with a footbridge over Bid Brook to our left. We, however, turned right on FP414 at the side of the field with the grounds of Hall Place (known locally as the Deer Park) on our right. The path is enclosed by a hedge at the end, with the gatehouse to our left and the wide gates to Hall Place on our right. We followed the path through the churchyard of the 13th century church, and down the steps to the main road.

7. We crossed the road to the spacious village green, including the cricket field, and admired the variety of differing architectural styles of the houses surrounding the green. We then walked along the side road with the school on the right and green on our left, past the village hall and through a modern housing estate to Lower Green Rd by the railway station. We walked under the railway bridge and past the oast houses of Paul's Farm on our right, as far as Paul's Hill House, where we turned right along FP422, to Penshurst Park. This is part of the Eden Valley Walk, which runs from Tonbridge to Haxted on the Surrey Border. We walked through an avenue of trees known as Martin's Drive with views of the house on our left (open to the public during summer months), as far as a sign for FP422 appeared on our right. This path took us through woodland, up and down a small valley till it emerged at the edge of the park by some cottages at Park Farm.

Leigh Park Farm

8. We crossed the C297 road and took the minor road, Cinder Hill (D299) opposite. When this road turned right over the railway, we followed the driveway to Little Moorden straight ahead (FP419), crossed a stile on our right and walked through the fields of Little Moorden where the last vestiges of hop poles were still to be seen to the buildings of Moorden. We turned right on the main road, and then took the Station Approach Road on our left, opposite a recently renovated oast house, which returned us to Penshurst Station.

2. Across the Bourne Valley

Circular Walk from Dene Park (Shipbourne)

(6 Miles)

OS Explorer Map 147

Grid REF: TQ 605 511

1. This walk starts from the Forestry Commission's car park at Dene Park, which is located in Puttenden Road, off Shipbourne Road (A227), between Tonbridge and Shipbourne. The nearest bus routes are numbers 222 (Tunbridge Wells/Wrotham) and 404 (from Sevenoaks).

2. From the car park, we followed the footpath through the wood parallel to Puttenden Road. The path emerged at the end of the wood, to a blind corner in Puttenden Road. We crossed the road and followed a tree-lined footpath, MT113, to a junction of footpaths where we turned left. We ignored a fire break on our left and entered a footpath just inside the edge of woodland with open fields on the right. When our path emerged from the woodland we followed the outside edge of the wood until we reached the point when the footpath went diagonally right across an open field with spectacular views over the Bourne Valley to a stile. We crossed a second field to a footbridge on the Bourne River. We then turned left, passed under an electricity pylon to Hampton Road, opposite a fish farm.

3. We turned left along Hampton Road until we reached Popes Villa Farm where we took an enclosed footpath diagonally right at the side of the farm. When we reached a kissing gate on our left we followed FP MR 376 to Puttenden Road at Dunks Green. We crossed

this road through a kissing gate to FP373 (part of the Greensand Way). We crossed a stile on our left, and ignoring a footpath on our right, we crossed a field diagonally on FP MR 380 to a wood. We entered the wood by a stile and followed the path straight through to the other side of the wood, at another stile across an arable field to School Lane.

Dunks Green pub (Kentish Rifleman)

4. We crossed this road, and followed the path at the side of a farm road, past the farm buildings of Fairlawn Home Farm. Our path carried ahead to a road at Shipbourne Common. We admired the various architectural designs of the houses in this area before crossing the Ightham Common Road (A227–continuation of Shipbourne Road). The notable buildings here are the Chaser Inn and the parish church of St Giles, rebuilt in 1722.

5. We walked through the churchyard to a junction of paths where we turned left. Our path then turned diagonally right across an arable field, over a ditch stream to another junction of paths. Here, we turned left on FP MR399 along a line of willows, and then diagonally right to a yellow post at the side of a copse. We kept to the left edge of the copse, and then, across an open field via a gate and footbridge to Hildenborough Road. We turned right in this road and opposite a signpost, we took FP MR402 through a gap in the hedge. Past the

side of a paddock, we reached a junction of paths. We turned left along an enclosed footpath (MR 400) and entered Kiln Wood. Our path led through the woods to a lay-by on the A227 road. We turned right in the lay-by, and crossed the road to re-enter Kiln Wood by a bridleway (MR 597). Just past a pond, we reached a junction of paths where we turned right, and walked straight ahead to the edge of the wood. On our way we noticed an old milestone which suggested that before the days of tarmac roads this bridleway would have been a main thoroughfare. Our way followed this bridleway until we reached the driveway to a private lane, where we turned right along a footpath at the edge of the woods, back to the Forestry Commission's car park.

Shipbourne Church

3. Where to Meet an Ostler

Walk from Otford to Shoreham and Return

(5 Miles)

OS Explorer Map 147

Grid REF: TQ525594

1. The walk starts from the car park at the sports ground. It can also be easily accessed by the London-Bromley-Swanley-Sevenoaks rail route or by the local Sevenoaks/Swanley bus route. Opposite the car park is the Heritage Centre Local Museum.

2. From the car park we walked diagonally right across the sports ground to a stile in the far corner. From here, we turned left along a gravel track (BW32). Where this track bent left, we kept straight on along what was now a tree-lined footpath with a golf course on either side. We crossed a junction at a narrow track (BW16), and followed what is now part of the Darenth Valley long distance path. This path emerged at a cricket ground from where we had our first sighting of the chalk cross that was carved in the hillside above Shoreham Village as a memorial to the members of the armed forces who had lost their lives during the First World War. In the Second World War, this cross had to be camouflaged so as not to provide a landmark for the German bombers. We followed the right hand edge of the cricket ground to an iron kissing gate. We passed through this, and continued the path to the road which runs from Shoreham village to the local railway station.

3. We turned left in this road, and opposite Shoreham Place, we turned right along FP4. At the wooden kissing gate on our left, we passed through the

churchyard of St Peter and St Paul's Church on a paved path. The 800-year-old church is notable for its impressive porch, the entrance of which was carved from an oak tree in the churchyard, a wall clock donated by a local pub and a pulpit originally housed in Westminster Abbey.

Otford Pickmoss door

4. We emerged from the churchyard to Church Street with the Olde George Inn on our left. The road crossed the River Darenth and passed the King's Arms Pub, which is notable for one of the very few remaining ostler's boxes, complete with the effigy of an ostler inside. The landscape hereabouts was popular with several well-known artists such as Samuel Palmer who considered the daylight here to be of superior quality to enhance their paintings. Church Street emerges at a T-junction, with Filston Lane to the left and the High Street to the right. We followed the High Street past the aircraft museum on our left, and turned left uphill on FP5 (The Landway).

Shoreham ostler's box

5. From here, we climbed up the side of the valley and passed the memorial cross on our right, to the edge of Meenfield Wood. Here we turned left and followed the hedge line on our left. Through gaps in the hedge, we gained spectacular views across the other side of the valley. After passing through a metal kissing gate

at the end of this path, we turned steeply downhill to Filston Lane.

6. We crossed this road and walked down Water Lane (FP16) to Kennel Cottage on our left. At the end of the road, the path continued to the side of a stream, crossed a footbridge and passed on our right an impressive-looking converted watermill. We walked uphill, passing Home Farm until we reached the edge of the golf course.

7. Here, we turned right on FP17 (part of the Darenth Valley walk), and passed through a tree-lined avenue until the path emerged at open farmland. We passed Lower Barn on our right, ignoring FP729 to our left and our path then followed the river – passing some allotment gardens on our left until we reached the main road at Otford. Just before this point, we noticed a house, where the river ran directly under it.

8. We turned left on the road (originally part of the Pilgrims' Way), and passed a number of impressive medieval timber-framed houses. The most notable of these is probably Pickmoss House. Our walk ended at the car park on the left opposite the Heritage Centre.

Otford mural

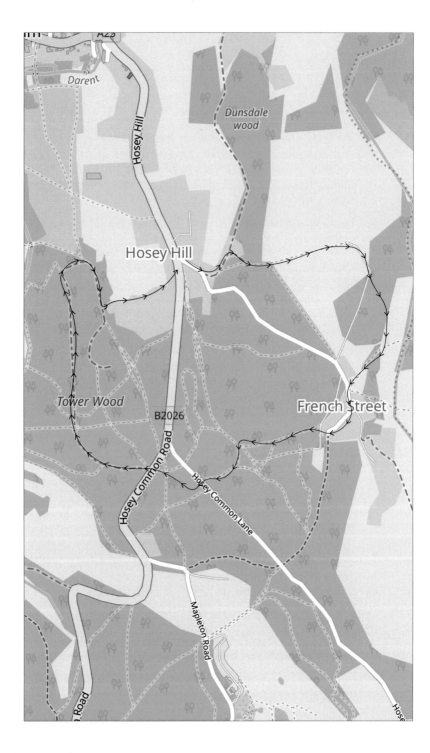

4. So, Why Build a Tower in the Middle of a Wood?

Circular Walk from Hosey Hill (Westerham)

(4 miles)

OS Explorer Map 147

Grid REF: TQ 453531

1. The start of the walk is best accessed by car. There is an occasional bus service (236) between East Grinstead Westerham and Oxted. Otherwise, the start point is approximately one mile up Hosey Hill from Westerham.

2. From the car park outside the old school house, we headed in the direction of Westerham to the junction of Hosey Common Rd and Hosey Common Lane (signposted to French Street). We turned right along Hosey Common Lane and after approximately 100 yards where the road turns right, we followed a driveway (FP306) at South Lodge. Before the house, we forked right through the woodland.

3. On our right hand side, we passed a gated batcave, which Kent Wildlife Trust occasionally opens to the public. Our path continued through woodland, and after the junction with FP385 on our right, the enclosed path opened out with fields and paddocks on either side. We then passed through a gate and circled a house to the left. We followed the path downhill, with iron railings on our left and Valence Woods on our right.

4. At the bottom of the valley, we turned right alongside a stream until we reached a row of steps on our left. We followed the path up the steps to the edge of the

woodland. This path would have continued to Piper's Green, but we turned diagonally right down through woodland along FP307 until we reached a footbridge over the stream to the right of a yellow waymark. After crossing the stream, we passed through a kissing gate, and followed the hedge line of an open field to another kissing gate. Our path then led uphill with open fields on our left until we reached the hamlet of French Street.

5. From the hillside at French Street, there are spectacular views over the valley towards Toys Hill. To our right, we noticed an enclosed private burial ground of Mr George Berry of St James's Street, London.

6. We turned left on the road at French Street and then right, at a house called Mannings Wood, onto a service road (BW375). Where this BW turned left, we carried straight on along FP382, which led to another service road, where we turned left and followed past a house called 'The Orchard' on our left, and entered woodland. We ignored all side paths until we reached a left/right fork. We took the right fork, which led to Hosey Common Lane. We turned right in the lane for a short distance before taking FP384 on our left. We followed this path, ignoring side turnings until we reached Hosey Common Road.

7. We crossed this road, and ignoring FP352 on our right, we entered Tower Wood, using the permissive path of the Squerryes Estate. We kept to the left path until we reached the ruined and ivy clad tower. The purpose of this three-storey tower is uncertain, and legend has it that the original owner had it built so that from the top, he could see St Paul's Cathedral. It is perhaps more likely that it would have been a hunting lodge or simply a folly.

Tower in Tower Wood

8. We followed the path downhill from the tower until we reached FP352 at the bottom and walked right through woodland. We passed the terraced gardens of Charts Edge on our left. These gardens are occasionally open to the public under the National Gardens Scheme. We turned left at the waymark on to a short boardwalk. At the next junction, we turned left, on to another short boardwalk on FP387, with the gardens on our left until the car park at Hosey Common Road.

5. Following the Pilgrims

Walk from Guildford to Chilworth

(6 Miles)

OS Explorer Map 145

Grid REF: TQ 893 497

1. This walk starts at Guildford Station, where there are frequent train services. There are public car parks in the town, but it might be better to use the park-and-ride scheme.

2. From the station, we crossed under the subway to the buildings by the River Wey. We found a gap between the buildings to the river bank, and turned right. On the other side of the river is Dupdine Wharf – a relic from the days when rivers and canals were used as the main means of transporting heavy freight. We noticed the sculpture of a bargeman of this period.

3. We continued along the paved river bank as far as a wide footbridge over the river. At this point, the pavement gives way to a grassy footpath, which continues at the side of the river. Lewis Carroll, the author of *Alice in Wonderland* and *Alice Through the Looking Glass* lived in Guildford for a while, and a model has been erected of Alice reading a book and the rabbit entering the rabbit hole. We continued walking along the tow-path with water meadows on the other side of the river.

4. Just before we reached a footbridge over the river, we passed the point where the Pilgrims Way from Winchester to Canterbury arrived at the old ferry crossing. On the hillock, by the ferry crossing, are the ruins of St Catherine's Chapel – restored in the 14th century to take advantage of the passing pilgrims. Local legend has it that when St Catherine and St

Martha were building their chapels, they only had one hammer between them, so they threw the hammer across the valley to one another to assist in the building work.

5. John Bunyan, the author of *The Pilgrim's Progress* lived near Shalford for a while and it has been suggested that when surveying the local scene, he was inspired to invent some of his allegories. Thus, pilgrims taking the ferry crossing were like Bunyan's character Pilgrim crossing the River Styx. The water meadows could have been the Slough of Despond. Fairs were held here to fleece the passing pilgrims, so this might have been Vanity Fair.

6. We crossed the footbridge over the river and re-traced our steps a few yards to where a footpath turned off at a right angle until it reached the main A281 road. We walked along the B road opposite until the point at which it turned diagonally left. Here, we crossed the road and followed the wide footpath (part of the North Downs Way) through Chantries Wood. This footpath emerged at Halfpenny Lane, where we turned left for a few yards, and then, right up the long sandy path to the top of St Martha's Hill. Here is St Martha's Chapel (the parish church of Chilworth). Although the chapel is located on the route of the Pilgrims Way, Norman stonework in the building suggests that the chapel was built before the murder of Thomas Becket and the subsequent pilgrims' route. The chapel was restored in the 19th century – rumoured to have been caused partially, at least by an unplanned gunpowder explosion from the gunpowder mills in the valley below. From the hilltop there are spectacular views over the countryside to the south.

7. We descended St Martha's Hill in the opposite direction to which we had climbed the hill. Just before the footpath reached the car park in Guildford Lane, we followed a narrow footpath on our right until it reached a T-junction, where we turned left and followed the path through woodland with the River

Tillingbourne below. This path emerged at millponds, at what would have been Albury Mill. Where the service road reached a T-junction, we turned right past a small, modern housing development and followed an enclosed footpath to two open fields. We crossed these to a wide footpath (part of the North Downs Way). Opposite, we took the permissive path at the side of the River Tillingbourne past the abandoned gunpowder mills. They ceased production soon after the end of the First World War. A display board at the entrance to the site explains the history of the mills.

St Catherine's Chapel

8. We followed the permissive path at the side of the river until we reached a picnic site. Here, we turned left, crossed a footbridge over the river, and followed the footpath to the A road. At this point, we turned left, past Chilworth School to the Percy Arms PH (Lord Percy was the Duke of Northumberland and his heirs still own much of the land hereabouts) and the railway station opposite. From here, it is possible to return to Guildford by a short train journey.

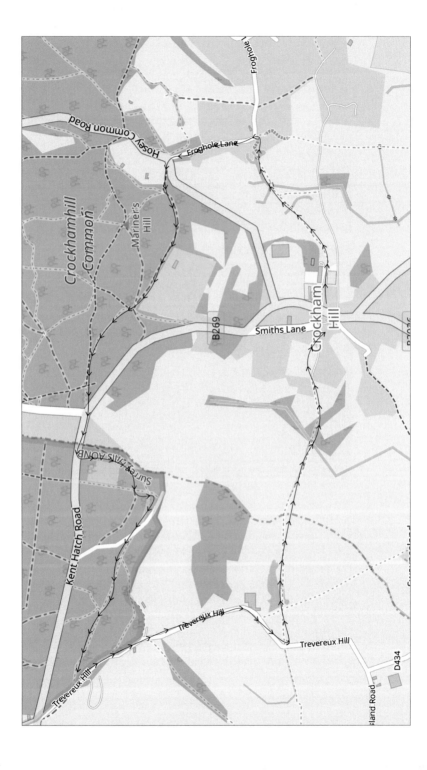

6. Octavia Hill's Legacy

Circular Walk from Crockham Hill

(4 Miles)

OS Explorer Map 147

Grid REF: TQ 428 490

1. Crockham Hill Village lies on the 236 bus route (East Grinstead/Edenbridge/Westerham/Oxted). There is ample car parking in the double car park next to the village hall off the B2026 road.

2. We started our walk at Holy Trinity Church next to the school. This church, constructed out of local sandstone, was built in 1842 as a curacy of St Mary's, Westerham. The church is replete with tokens of Octavia Hill, who was not only a joint founder of the National Trust, but was also a pioneer of social housing in the London East End. Inside the church is a marble effigy of Octavia and a window dedicated to her work. Outside in the churchyard are the graves of Octavia and her sister. Once a year, the Octavia Hill Society meets to commemorate her achievements.

3. We took FP377 from the end of the cul-de-sac approach, across open grazing fields. The ground is unstable here because it lies on the Greensand Ridge, and was the site of a minor earthquake in 1596. Our path crossed two fields, over a stream and up to the hamlet of Froghole. Before climbing Buttle Steps up to Froghole Lane, we paused to admire the view to our right over the Ashdown Forest and the South Downs. It is rumoured that the name, 'Froghole' originated from the frogs that used to congregate around the many springs in this area.

4. On reaching the top of the steps at Froghole Lane, we turned left and noticed the precipice below the road.

(This may have been caused by the minor earthquake). At the end of the lane, we crossed Hosey Common Road (B2026), and followed BW362 across Crockham Hill Common. Ignoring all side paths, we followed the bridleway until it emerged at a clearing with three houses on our left. One of these was Larkswood (the home of Octavia Hill) and another, the gardener's house. During the summer, the gardens of all three houses are opened to the general public on specified dates under the National Gardens Scheme.

Octavia Hill's tomb

5. Just past these houses, we reached a footpath junction with a signpost. Here we turned right and then immediately left along FP362 (part of the Greensand Way) through woodland. This path met another path coming in from the right and we continued straight on until we reached a waymark, Greensand Way and Limpsfield circular walk, where we turned diagonally left to the B269 road at the junction with Goodley Stock Road at Kent Hatch. Here we enjoyed more spectacular views across the same vista as we had seen earlier. We walked a short distance along the B269 road and just before a traffic sign indicating the Kent/Surrey

border, we turned left along a tarmac driveway (FP G46) of a house called 'Greystones'. This driveway gave way to a path through woodland where our path met a T-junction. We turned left, down FP G45 (part of the Tandridge Border Path) to another tarmac driveway. Here, we turned right and then turned left through more woodland on FP G48 (running parallel to Kent Hatch Road) until we emerged at the top of Trevereux Hill (BW G49, part of the Vanguard Way), opposite what would have been the old school house; the bell tower provides a clue.

6. We walked downhill to the bottom where Trevereux Manor lay on our left and the houses that would originally have been tithe cottages on our right. Here, we turned left, opposite the cottages onto FP G51 into a grazing field. This allowed us to get a good sight of Trevereux Manor, which following a fire, has largely been rebuilt under the auspices of Richard Stilgoe and incorporates a children's music centre. We followed our path at the side of the field into a second field and over a stream into a copse. The path is now designated FP370 because it has re-entered the county of Kent. We walked up through the copse into a grazing field and walked uphill to a lane between two large detached houses. Here, we turned right until we came to Smiths Lane. We turned right again and emerged at Crockham Hill Village centre, opposite the village garden. We noticed here an ornate village sign, again commemorating Octavia Hill, and a slate memorial to the staff and children of a London orphanage, who were evacuated to Weald House on Hosey Common Road to escape the German bombing in the Second World War. Tragically Weald House was bombed by a German aircraft with massive loss of life. The victims were buried with a remembrance stone in Edenbridge Cemetery, next to the parish churchyard.

7. We turned left in the main road, and then right down to the car park by the village hall.

7. In Search of the Chiding Stone

Circular Walk from Chiddingstone Causeway (Penshurst Station) via Chiddingstone Village

(5 miles)

OS Explorer Map 147

Grid REF: TQ 519 464

1. This walk can be accessed either from Penshurst Station on the Redhill-Tonbridge railway line or by the 231/233 bus route between Edenbridge and Tunbridge Wells. Car parking is available on the station approach road on the south side of the station.

Village post office

2. Chiddingstone Causeway Village came into being as a result of the construction of the railway line in the 19th century. Rather confusingly the station is called Penshurst, although the village of Penshurst, built around Penshurst Place, is situated two miles away. The two main features of Chiddingstone Causeway are the former cricket ball factory (since shut due largely as a result of cheaper products from Asia) and St Luke's Church. This church was built in the late 19th century to the design of John Bentley, the same architect who designed the Roman Catholic Cathedral at Westminster.

3. We started our walk from the gate next to the timber yard on the south side of the station. We followed FP493 by the right hand edge of a field. This path led into a second field, where we reached a T-junction of footpaths. Here, we turned left until we reached a gate. After passing through this gate and crossing a stile in the next field, we turned left along FP490. At the end of this field, we turned right over a stile on FP492. We followed this path with a hedge on our left and at the corner we followed the path over a footbridge into another field. Here, we walked diagonally left to a waymark post at the end of another hedge. We followed the path (now FP499) at the side of the hedge to farm buildings at Sandholes. One of these buildings had the outline of what might have been a bakehouse.

4. At Sandholes, we crossed the D298 road into a farmyard and followed the path at the side of a hedge. We passed through a gate on our left and followed the same path, but now with the hedge on our right. At the end of this field, we exited right, and then kept left until we met FP498 coming in from our right. Here, we turned left on FP498, heading towards a farm gate at the opposite end of the field. As we walked along this field, we could see the tower of Chiddingstone Church in the distance, and on our right, the brick building which would originally have been the local poor house. After passing through the gate at the far end of this field, we followed the path along the right hand edge of the next field to a gate in the far corner. This led into a hard track (FP515) which crossed the River Eden just past the houses of Somerden Green, and then emerged at Chiddingstone High Street.

Chiddingstone Castle

5. We paused in the village to admire the many notable features. Chiddingstone Castle, the home of the Streatfield family for several centuries, was never built as a fortress, but more as a manor house. It was originally called High Street House, and the road was diverted to accommodate the construction of a lake. The present building was built in Gothic style. The property was purchased by an antiques' dealer called Denys Bower in 1955 to accommodate his collection of Stuart, Jacobite, Oriental and Egyptian artefacts. The following year, he opened his collection as a museum to the general public. He died in 1977 and bequeathed his property to the National Trust – but probably because there was no endowment with the bequest to cover ongoing maintenance – the National Trust declined the offer. Since then, a local trust has been created to maintain and enhance the property.

6. The row of medieval timbered and gabled houses at the side of the castle gate, including the Castle PH, were acquired by the National Trust in 1939. St Mary's Church was built in the 14th century, but was struck by lightning in 1624 – no lightning conductors in those

days – and not reopened until 1629. Features of the church include an elaborate 'spider' brass chandelier and a lectern bible with the word 'vineyard' misprinted as 'vinegar'. Behind the High Street lies the Chiding Stone, a large rock in the shape of a pulpit. Several legends narrate the purpose of this rock. One local legend was that it was the place where ancient Druids worshipped. Another more prosaic legend was that it was where husbands whipped their recalcitrant wives.

7. Resuming our walk, we passed along the High Street, away from the village. We walked past the overflow churchyard and Larkins Farm (the home of Larkins Brewery) on our left, to a T-junction with an oast house in the middle of the road. We turned right in the road for a few yards, then left, at the side of a pond along a footpath across an arable field. At the T-junction of paths at the end of this field, we turned left and out of the field through a clump of trees down to the driveway of Vexour. We turned left in the driveway and walked down to the road by Vexour Bridge over the River Eden. Immediately after crossing the bridge, we turned right into a field where we were confronted with a choice of two paths. We took FP490 to our right and entered the field by a footbridge over a ditch stream. Again, we were confronted with a choice of two paths. We followed FP491 to our right, crossed two more ditch streams, and headed diagonally left to a stile. We then walked on to where two paths joined (FPs 491 and 492). We took the left path (FP492) over another ditch stream and emerged at the junction of the B2176 road, and the Station Approach Road at Moorden. We then followed the Approach Road back to our starting point at Penshurst Station.

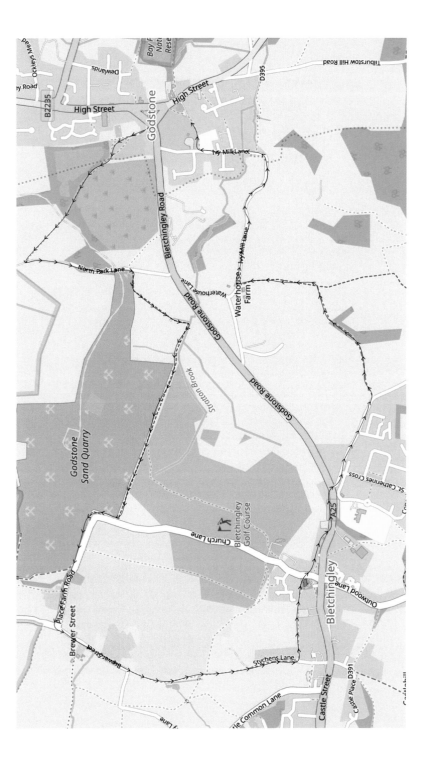

8. Where Archbishop Desmond Tutu First Preached

Circular Walk from Godstone to Bletchingley and Return

(5 miles)

OS Explorer Map146

Grid REF: TQ 348517

1. This walk is best accessed by Caterham/Redhill (400) and Redhill/Hurst Green (410) buses. There are two car parks on the green from where the walk starts.

2. From the green, we crossed the A25 at the side of the Hare & Hounds PH, and took the footpath between houses to a kissing gate on our left. This led diagonally left and slightly upwards towards a wooded area. A windmill is reputed to have stood in this field at one time. An enclosed path with high security fence led through the wooded area. The land on either side of the security fences was designated for the East Surrey Water Company and a local diving club – must be some connection there. This path emerged at a service road, which we crossed and walked over an open grazing field to North Park Lane on the opposite side. At this point, we had our first view of the M25 and the North Downs beyond.

3. This section of the road is a public bridleway, and we turned left towards the A25. This took us past an access road to the sandpits on our right. Shortly afterwards, we turned right along another bridleway at North Park Cottages. This bridleway was, in fact, a long diversion around the sandpits, which eventually emerged at Church Lane. The bridleway followed next to the road for a while and when the bridleway ended, we continued along Church Lane, passing Place Farm

on our right. This was formerly the site of Bletchingley Manor, the ancestral home of the Dukes of Buckingham. Church Lane ended at a T-junction, where we turned left along Brewer Street. As we headed south towards Bletchingley, we admired on our right the fine timberframe building of Brewer Street Farmhouse. After passing a small industrial estate on our left, the road bent sharp right but we carried straight on along a public footpath. Where this path met a service road, we kept to the left of this road, and after passing a few houses on our left, we turned sharp left towards the churchyard of St Mary, the Virgin Church in Bletchingley Village. We paused to admire the view of the North Downs beyond the M25.

Brewer Street farmhouse

4. The church, with its crenellated tower and walls, has a number of significant features including the imposing early Norman tower, the sculptured monument of Sir Robert Clayton and his wife (interestingly designed by himself and carved in his lifetime) and to the west of the pulpit was a portrait of Archbishop Desmond Tutu, who was a curate at this church from 1965 to 1967.

5. We admired the rich texture of picturesque buildings in the High Street and Church Walk, the most notable of which is probably the old coaching inn of the Whyte Harte. The wide High Street perhaps signifies its earlier importance as a Coach Road and a market town. To the south of the High Street lay the foundations of the Norman Castle situated on the top of Castle Hill. Bletchingley was notorious for being one of the so called 'rotten' parliamentary boroughs that were expunged by the 1832 Reform Bill. Until that time just eight electors held the privilege of electing two MPs to the House of Commons.

6. From the churchyard, we turned right into Church Lane, and then took the public footpath between houses to the A25. Here, we turned left, passed the Bletchingley Arms PH and crossed the road to take a path next to the road that led to a modern housing estate at the junction with Rabies Heath Road. We walked along this road for about half a mile, and where the road bent right, we took a footpath on the opposite side of the road that led through a copse into a grazing field. We kept to the left hand side of this field into a dip where we turned left alongside woodland. This path curved round to the right and emerged into another grazing field. When the footpath came to a T-junction, we turned left, past the farm building of Water House Farm to Ivymill Lane.

7. We turned right here and followed the road past the gatehouse of Garston Park to a left bend in the road, where we took a footpath on our left on an embankment. We walked past the site of what would have been Ivymill Water Mill at a time when the river would have had a greater flow of water than it has now. Our path re-joined Ivymill Lane and after passing the village school on our right, we reached the village green, where we turned right to return to the car park from where we had started our walk.

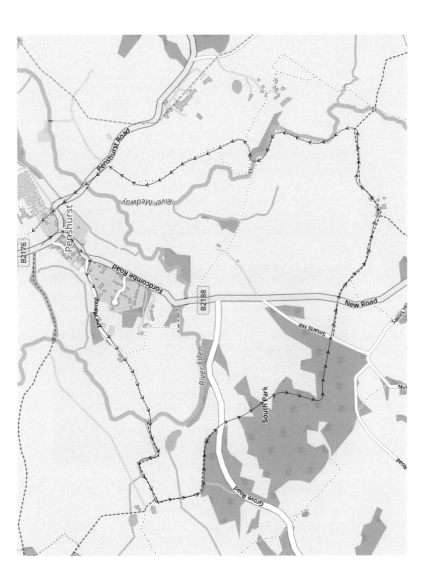

9. On the Dole in Penshurst

Circular Walk from Penshurst

(6 Miles)

OS Explorer Map 147

Grid REF: TQ 526438

1. Penshurst Village lies on the 231/233 bus routes between Edenbridge and Tunbridge Wells. (Penshurst Station is located two miles away at Chiddingstone Causeway). Car parking is available in the lay-by at the side of the B2176 road, opposite the grounds of Penshurst Place or in the field car park at Penshurst Place.

Leicester Square, Penshurst

2. We walked to the Village Hall at the corner of the High Street and turned right along the High Street, past the petrol station (formerly, the Village Blacksmith) to the school. Here, we turned right along the Warren (FP441). This road extended as far as what was Warren Farm. At this point, the path became a grassy track

which led across two fields to a footbridge over the River Eden. We followed the path through a wooded area at the side of a stream before passing through a kissing gate and around two sides of a grazing field.

3. We then reached Harden Cottage where we followed a circuitous diversion around three sides of this property before returning to the line of the original path. At least, the diversion allowed us to see the millpond and array of oast houses at Salman's Farm, an indication that, at one time, these fields would have been covered with hops. Our path now entered the north side of the vineyard. At the far end, we entered a copse and at a footpath junction turned left down FP442. This path led to the south side of the vineyard, and then right to a footbridge. We walked diagonally left over a grazing field, over another footbridge and uphill until we climbed through a copse to the C306 road (The Grove).

Oast houses

4. We crossed this road and walked up a very worn set of stone steps called the Monks Steps into a field where we walked diagonally left, past a clump of trees to the side fence of South Park Farm/Horns Lodge. We followed this path to a gate and then walked around two sides of an extended garden to a driveway where we turned right to Coldharbour Road at the side of the

Bottle House Pub. We turned left in the road, and then almost immediately turned right along an enclosed path (FP460) to Nunnery Lane. Here we turned left to a crossroads where we took the right turn to Smarts Hill and the Spotted Dog PH on the edge of a precipice or landslip. Among the row of houses by the pub is a former chapel since converted into a private residence.

5. Before we took FP459 on our left in a gap between the houses, we paused to admire the spectacular view across the Medway Valley to Swaylands. We walked downhill to the Penshurst-Fordcombe Road (B2188) and took FP459 almost opposite to a farm driveway (BW458). Here, we turned right and followed the driveway to the farm buildings of Nash's Farm and the junction with BW467. We turned left along the original BW and walked between the rows of hedges to a gate and stile just short of the River Medway. At this stage, we turned sharp left on FP454 around two edges of an arable field with the river to our right. This path led into a second field, still with the river on our right, until we reached a foot bridge over the river. Ignoring FP450 to our left, we crossed the footbridge and followed the path round the left-hand edge of another arable field, on which old hop poles gave an indication of what the fields would have been used for, to a T-junction of paths at the end. We took FP449 to our left, walking parallel to the river and noticed the point where the River Eden ran into the River Medway. Our path eventually emerged to the road at Rogue's Hill, opposite the Village Almshouses. We walked down the road towards Penshurst Village and crossed two river bridges. By the first bridge is a private house formerly called the Bridge Tavern PH.

6. We reached the village at the entrance to Penshurst Place and walked up a few steps to the original Leicester Square. (The Leicester Square in the London West End is the second square of that name because it was the London residence of the Earl of Leicester.) One of the buildings in the Square is the Old Guild House

which in earlier days was an alehouse called Ye Olde Kings Head. In the churchyard in front of the church porch is one of the remaining dole tables. In medieval times, items of food and clothing were laid out here on certain religious festivals for the benefit of the poor of the parish. The more notable features of the sandstone-built church include an imposing square tower with battlements, turrets, the Sidney Chapel with its monuments to the Sidney family and a brightly painted vault decorated with heraldic shields.

Dole Table, Penshurst churchyard

7. We walked through the churchyard to the left of the church tower and emerged into a field at the side of Penshurst Place. Here, we walked diagonally left on FP430, back to the lay-by on the B2176 Road.

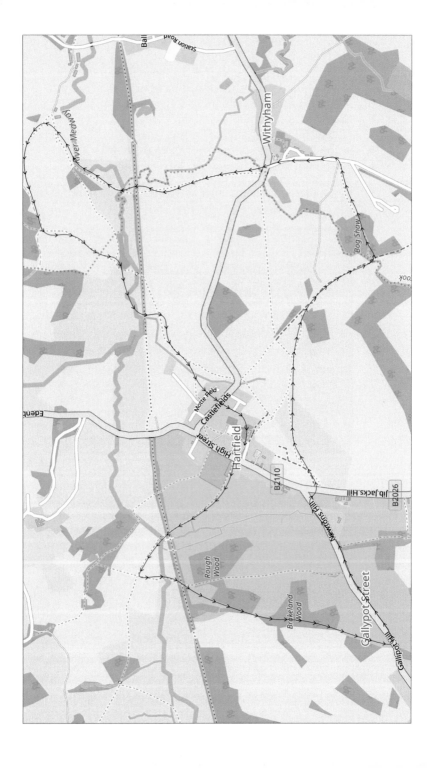

10. The Domain of the Sackvilles

Circular Walk from Hartfield

(5 Miles)

OS Explorer Map 135

Grid REF: TQ 476 358

1. The car park in Hartfield is at the side of the village green. The public transport link is the 291 bus (Tunbridge Wells/Crawley).

2. From the car park, we walked back along the service road and crossed the village High Street (B2026). We passed the sports ground on our left and ignoring a gate on our right we passed a wide bridleway gate where we took the path to our left. We then walked through two fields with a hedge on our right. This led to a wooden gate and a brick bridge over the disused single track railway line that ran through East Grinstead, Forest Row and Groombridge (now a designated cycle track named 'The Forest Way'). Our path then took us over a footbridge, crossing the River Medway (quite narrow at this point) and into woodland.

3. At a path junction with a waymark, we turned left and soon emerged from the woodland to an open field. We continued at the left hand edge of the field, over a footbridge crossing the river and under a railway bridge to a gate leading into woodland. After our path emerged from the woodland, we followed through the farmyard of Culver's Farm. This path took us through to Newton's Hill (B2110).

4. We turned left in this road to the junction with Jib Jack's Hill (B2026) and admired the village sign at the end of the High Street. We crossed Jib Jack's Hill to a sign posted, 'footpath' that followed around the left

hand edge of the field. In the next field we walked diagonally right to a stile in the far corner. Here, we were faced with a choice of two paths. We took the path, part of the Wealdway, that ran diagonally across the next field to a waymark in the far corner. We followed the direction of the waymark and passed Forstal Farm on our left. Our path left the field by a gate in the corner, over a river bridge and through a copse to a field at the lane (bridleway), leading left to the Withyam village, church of St Michael and All Angels.

Withyham Church

5. This church, which has been under the patronage of the Sackville family since the 16th century, was almost completely destroyed by a lightning blast in 1672. Probably the most striking feature of this Church is the Sackville Chapel, with its monument to the young Thomas Sackville. The monument depicts his parents, the fifth Earl and the Countess of Dorset, grieving over the death of their 13-year-old son. Other notable buildings in the village include the Old Rectory next to the church (a 14th century building with a Georgian facade) and Buckhurst Park, a 16th century house and the ancestral seat of the Sackville family. The countryside around here was the site of two medieval deer parks.

Withyham Church, Sackville memorial

6. From the Church, we walked down the lane to the B2110 road, crossed Hawkins Bridge on our left and crossed the main road to a stile. From here, we walked across two fields and then over the abandoned railway track. We then made for the footbridge over the River Medway into what has been designated a natural conservation area and then diagonally right to a stile in the corner of a field. We then climbed a narrow, uphill path to a footpath T-junction (part of the Weald-way). We turned left and walked parallel to the river until we reached another footpath T-junction. The path to the right would have led to Tophill Farm, but we turned left past the side of a pond and descended to a footbridge over the river and the abandoned railway track. We crossed over the stile opposite into a field, where we walked diagonally right to a gap in a hedge. We then turned right and walked alongside the hedge through two fields to a stile in the corner (FP23).

7. After crossing this stile, we followed the path past the site of what would have been a motte-and-bailey forti-fication to defend this section of the River Medway (Obviously, the river would have been much wider and navigable at that time). The site is reflected in the street names of the housing estate, through which we passed before crossing the B2110 road and walking across the village green where we had started our walk.

11. In the Steps of Charles Darwin

Walk from Cudham to Downe and Return

(5 Miles)

OS Explorer Map 147

Grid REF: TQ 447597

1. There is a car park at the sports ground in the centre of Cudham Village. There is also a bus link by the R10 Orpington/ Halstead route.

2. From the car park, we walked past the sports pavilion and turned left through the churchyard. The Church, constructed largely of flint, is mainly early-medieval with traces of Norman work. In the churchyard are two giant yew trees that pre-date the present Church building.

3. We crossed Cudham Lane and followed Church Hill Road to the left. We then took the footpath LB 267 on our right through a copse to an open valley with extensive views in all directions. We followed this path across the valley and up the other side through woodland to the hamlet of Single Street. Here, we crossed the road to the enclosed footpath directly opposite LB237A. When this path emerged into grazing fields, we turned right along the footpath LB237 to Birdhouse Lane by Luxted Farmhouse.

4. We turned right in the road, and then almost immediately turned left at the side of Northfield Cottage, on what was the continuation of footpath LB237. We followed this path straight between the grazing fields. At the far end, we kept to the left of the hedge and followed round the edge of a field, across a service road and to the left of farm buildings, at Downe Court. Our path emerged at an open field where we walked

diagonally across to a copse. At this point, we diverted slightly to cross Luxted Road and examine the exterior of Down House, the Victorian Country House, where for 40 years, Charles Darwin wrote some of his most famous books – including *The Origin of Species by Natural Selection* and studied the surrounding countryside. The house is now open to the general public under the auspices of English Heritage, who have tried to retain the fabric of the building as it was when Darwin lived there with his family.

Down House
Bottom right: Downe Church window

5. Returning to our footpath, we passed through a copse and followed the path at the side of a hedge to the rear of Christmas Tree Farm, an animal playground for young families. At the footpath junction, we turned left and followed the path to Luxted Road. Here, we turned right and followed the road to the centre of the village, at the parish Church of St Mary, the Virgin.

6. This medieval Church, constructed of flint, has had several restorations. The last of these was in 1950, following the destruction of much of the Church by a German flying bomb

in 1944. Among the more prominent features of the church are a large brass of Jacob Verzelinvi, a Venetian glass-maker and a stained glass window dedicated by the parents of Robin Knox Johnson in thanksgiving for the safe return of their son, following his solo circumnavigation of the world under sail without touching land. He left Falmouth in his yacht, Suhalli, in June, 1968, returning in April 1969 and having lost wireless communication with the outside world for several weeks. In the churchyard is a yew tree, which pre-dates the Church) and the graves of several of Darwin's family.

7. Leaving the churchyard, we exited the village along Cudham Road, past the front of Christmas Tree Farm, and were soon able to leave the road by taking the footpath LB238, which runs next to the road. When the path emerged further along Cudham Road, we crossed the road and followed the path at the side of houses down into Hangrove Wood (This is a part of Downe Bank Nature Reserve run by Kent Wildlife Trust). We walked down the steps past Orbis Bank, where Darwin discovered eight different varieties of orchids. We crossed the valley where there is a camp site in the fields next to the path. We climbed up the other side of the valley to a T-junction of footpaths. Here we turned left on a bridleway and emerged at a driveway leading to Cudham Lane North.

8. We turned left in this road, and just past Hostye Farm, we turned right along the footpath LB242. We walked across two fields to the road at Mace Lane. Looking behind us, we could see the buildings of Canary Wharf. We turned left in Mace Lane and then right along the footpath LB243. This path led through a copse and across two fields to a service road. Crossing this road, we emerged at the sports ground where we had started our walk.

12. When Hops Were Grown in Penshurst

Circular Walk from Penshurst

(6 Miles)

OS Explorer Map 147

Grid REF: TQ 526 438

1. Penshurst village lies on the 231/233 bus routes between Edenbridge and Tunbridge Wells. (Penshurst Station is located two miles away at Chiddingstone Causeway). Car parking is available in the lay-by at the side of the B2176, opposite the grounds of Penshurst Place, or in the field car park at Penshurst Place.

Penshurst Place

2. Penshurst Place is a mediaeval stately mansion and home to the Sidney family since 1552. Among the notable features, it is celebrated for its 14th century baronial hall and its ornamental gardens.

3. We walked up the road away from the village and past the lay-by, took byway 546 (locally known as the Coach Road or Court Green Lane) on our left. This is part of the Eden Valley walk. We crossed the River Eden, and at the junction of paths, took the right fork. As the path climbed slightly, we could admire the view over the Eden Valley and the cluster of oast houses in Chiddingstone Village. We passed Wat Stock (an old timber-framed building) on our left, at the junction with BW440 and FP438. Among the farm buildings on our right were some coloured walls which look as if they were designed to resemble buildings in a French vineyard. The view of this can best be appreciated at some distance away near Chiddingstone Village.

4. Past Wat Stock, the byway (now BW440) assumes a tarmac surface. After passing two ponds on our right, we went through a gate (which was also on our right) diagonally across a field to the C327 road. We crossed this road and took the byway 544 through woodland to a junction. We ignored FP518 on our right, which led to Chiddingstone Village, and carried onto the hamlet of Hill Hoath.

5. The byway wound between houses to the junction with the D297 road, where we turned left along BW531, and then left again along FP532 across grazing fields parallel to a horse jump course. Our path emerged at the end of the horse jump course and entered Stock Wood. After about 100 yards, the main path through the woods became FP533, but we turned left at a waymark post, and soon emerged from the woods into an open field. We crossed this field diagonally and exited the field in the left hand corner to Trugger's Gill. From this point, our path headed down hill and then uphill a little way. Keeping the fence on our left, we entered a field with a hedge on our left and entered an enclosed path through woodland, over a footbridge to the C337 road at Chiddingstone Hoath.

6. Here, we turned left to the centre of this small village at Hoath Corner and The Rock Public House, where

the owner of Larkins Brewery holds sway. At the road junction, we turned right for a few yards, and then followed left, past a few buildings into Puckden Wood on FP539. We took the right fork in the wood and emerged into an open field, which we crossed, and then turned sharp right at the side of a hedge. We then dropped down into the farm road at Oakenden, a timber-framed farmhouse which sports an impressive display of snowdrops in the New Year. We turned left in this farm road (FP544), and we passed to the right of the last building in this road to an open field. We followed the left hand edge of this field into the woods, where our path bent right and then left, ignoring FP442, which led to Grove Road.

7. Our path then entered a vineyard where we followed the hedge on our left to the point where our path had been officially diverted round three sides of Harden Cottage. The diverted path, at least, enabled us to appreciate what would possibly have been a mill pond and the oast houses at Salmans Farm. At the end of the diversion, we followed FP441 along the two sides of a field and then left at the side of a slip stream until we crossed a footbridge over the River Eden. This river joins the River Medway behind the Leicester Arms PH in Penshurst Village.

8. We then walked slightly uphill at the left hand edge of a field to buildings which would originally have been Warren Farm. At this point, the FP becomes a service road leading to Penshurst Village at the side of the school on to the B2188 road. We turned left in this road, passing the much photographed petrol station (formerly a blacksmith's) on our left to the village hall in the centre of the village. Here, we turned right to return to our starting point at the lay-by.

13. Bolebrooke – A Castle or a Manor House?

Another Circular Walk from Hartfield

(6 Miles)

OS Explorer Map 135

Grid REF: TQ 479358

1. The car park in Hartfield is at the side of the village green. The public transport link is the 291 bus (Tunbridge Wells/Crawley).

2. From the car park, we walked across the village green and over the B2110 road into the modern housing estate at Castle fields. At the side of the small car park at the far end of the estate, we crossed a stile into a field with the site of the motte-and-bailey on our left. We crossed this field diagonally to another stile, marked FP226. We then walked along the left hand edge of two grazing fields as far as a gap in the hedge. Here, we passed through the gap and walked diagonally across this next field to the disused railway track of the line that would previously have run from East Grinstead to Groombridge via Forest Row. This is now a designated cycle track called 'Forest Way'.

3. We crossed the old railway track, and then the footbridge over the River Medway to FP15. This path started to climb uphill and after passing a pond in a cluster of trees on our right, we reached a junction of paths. We took the path ahead and walked diagonally right uphill over arable fields to a copse in the far corner of the field. Before entering the copse, we paused to turn around to look behind us at Hartfield Village nestling in the valley below and Ashdown Forest beyond. We walked through the copse and then along an enclosed path, with grazing fields on our

left and the buildings of Top Hill Farm on our right. When this path ended at a gate, we walked diagonally left across a field to the entrance of a wood on FP74. We walked through the woods along the side of a field. Where the path turned right at a path junction, we took the left path uphill to the driveway of Perryhill Farm. This driveway took us past Perryhill Oast, the farm buildings of Perryhill Farm and Bolebroke Farm, emerging eventually at the B2026 road.

Bolebroke Castle gateway

4. We crossed this road, turned left and immediately right along a public bridleway sign posted to Bolebroke Castle. We passed the Perryhill Orchard Tea Rooms on our right and after the bridleway turned right, we had our first view of the extensive moat of Bolebroke Castle. Our path turned left and then right, towards the imposing gatehouse, of what was probably a medieval manor house. The gatehouse is the only remnant of this building.

5. We passed the gatehouse on our right and our path, FP42C, followed a straight line through Coomb Wood and fields until we reached a T-junction of paths. We took the left path (FP50B) past Chantner's Farm and through a copse before emerging into an open grazing field. In the distance on our right, we could see the church tower at East Grinstead. We followed the left hand hedge of the field along two sides, before dropping down to the farmyard of Bassett's Manor now riding stables and a collection of small industrial units. A driveway led through the yard and out to the public road at Butcherfield Lane.

6. We turned left in this lane and when the road turned sharp left, we took a footpath on our right. Almost immediately, we met a junction of paths where we took a bridleway on our left, going downhill and passing Chantner's Farm on our left. At a path junction, we turned right along BW376 and soon emerged into open fields. We followed this path, with a hedge on our left, as far as a cross path – part of the High Weald Landscape Trail. We turned left at this point and walked across a field to a footbridge over the River Medway. We then crossed the disused railway track again, diagonally left across a field to the far side where we turned left and followed the path with a hedge on our right until we reached the sports ground.

7. We emerged from the sports ground into Hartfield High Street with its assortment of attractive medieval houses of varying designs and histories. Probably the most patronised building is *Pooh Corner Shop*, selling trinkets associated with A. A. Milne's stories about Winnie the Pooh. A. A. Milne lived near here inter-mittently, and Pooh Bridge is located in the nearby Ashdown Forest – the setting for many of the stories.

8. We turned right in the High Street and then left, along Church Street, past the Anchor PH to the two-storey, timber-framed cottage, which not only accommodated the Church verger and his family, but also doubled as the lych-gate. We passed through the churchyard, visiting the early medieval Church with its shingled spire and impressive, modern stained-glass window, passing the side of the school to the car park and village green where we had begun our walk.

Hartfield Church lych gate

14. Is This the Oldest Yew Tree?

Walk from South Godstone to Crowhurst and Return

(5 Miles)

OS Explorer Map 146

Grid REF: TQ 362483

1. This walk is best accessed on the Redhill-Tonbridge railway line. The village also lies on the 409 bus route (East Grinstead-Selsdon).

2. From Godstone Station, we turned right along the A22 road and passed under a railway bridge. We crossed the road to a stile opposite, and followed the footpath through a series of grazing fields parallel to the railway line, ignoring side paths on left or right until we reached Tandridge Lane at the hamlet of Crowhurst Lane End.

3. We walked along the road at Crowhurst Lane End and just before the road bent left, we turned right, just past a house called Rozel, down an enclosed footpath. We crossed two stiles and a footbridge over a ditch stream to emerge at an open grazing field. We crossed this field diagonally left to the entrance to the woodlands of Ashen Plantation. We followed a broad footpath through the woods until we emerged at open grazing fields, where we walked straight on with hedges to our left until we reached the churchyard of St George's Church at Crowhurst.

4. Parts of this small Church were built in the 12th or 13th century, but restoration work was required in the 17th and 19th centuries. The most notable feature of this Church, however, lies in the churchyard. Here is a giant yew tree – now supported by stakes, which has been certified as over 4,000 years old. The centre of the

trunk is hollow and so wide that it has been claimed that on one occasion, there was enough space for a dozen parishioners to sit here around a table. There is even a small wooden gate that would once have been the entrance to the hollowed-out trunk. Opposite the churchyard is a late medieval farmhouse, now called Mansion House Farm, formerly the manor house of the Angell family.

Crowhurst Church

5. We retraced our steps into the field before the church-yard, and walked diagonally across the field to a gap in the hedge opposite. We then walked diagonally left to a stile and an enclosed path which led out to a farm road, where we turned right towards Stocks/ Kingswood Farms. We then turned right through the farm buildings to an open grazing field. We crossed this field to enter the woodlands at Ashen Plantation again. The path through the woods led us to where we had entered the woods earlier in the walk. Confronted with two stiles, we took the left one and crossed two

paddock fields to a stile and footbridge. Our path then took us around the left of a fishing lake and over a stile into Tandridge Lane.

6. On this road, we turned right for a few yards and then left along a bridleway at Lagham Lodge Farm. When this tarmac farm road gave out, we continued in the same direction through the grazing fields with fencing on our right. At the end of these fields, we passed through a gate to an enclosed path which wound round to the right. When the path met a junction, we took the enclosed path on our left. This path opened out on to a grazing field, where we aimed for the corner of a copse. We walked to the right of a hedge and then across the field to a gate. After passing through another gate, we noticed on our left (in woodland) the extensive remains of Lagham Manor. This fortified manor house was built by Roger de St John (a knight and powerful member of the court of Henry III), using the basis of earlier earthworks in 1262. The lord and all his household were subsequently wiped out by the Black Death. The original manor house was succeeded by the construction of a Jacobean house in 1662. Our path followed two sides of this moat until we reached the farm buildings of Lagham Manor Farm. After passing between the farm buildings, we followed the service road to the A22, where we turned right to return to the railway station and bus stop at South Godstone.

The Crowhurst Yew

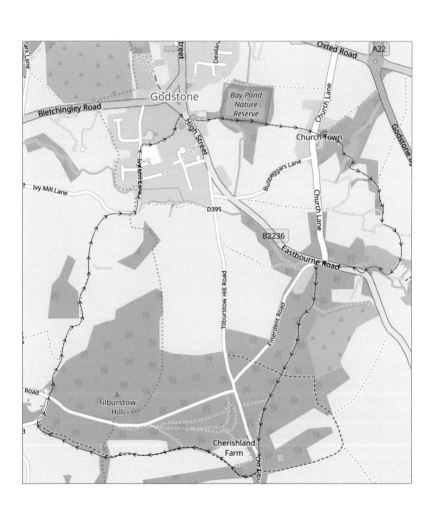

15. To See the Final Resting Place of Walker Miles

Circular Walk from Godstone

(5 Miles)

OS Explorer Map 146

Grid REF: TQ 3485l7

1. This walk is best accessed by Caterham/Redhill (400) and Redhill/Oxted/Hurst Green (410) buses. There are car parks on the green from where the walk starts.

White Hart, Godstone

2. From the car park, we crossed Tilburstow Hill Road to the White Hart PH opposite (formerly a coaching inn and said to date from the time of Richard II) where William Cobbett, the author, stayed for a while when he was writing his commentary on the British country-side, 'Rural Rides'. We followed the public footpath at the side of the inn, past the Village Hall, and then the Bay Pond on our left. This pond was created to power the gunpowder mills but is now a nature reserve tended by the Surrey Wildlife Trust.

3. This path emerged at Church Lane, which we crossed to the churchyard of St Nicholas' Church. To the right of the churchyard is a small group of alms houses, designed by Sir George Gilbert Scott, complete with a chapel and a well. We followed the path through the churchyard and noticed on our left a rough headstone marking the grave of Edmund Seyfang Taylor. He was a book publisher in London, and was affectionately known as Walker Miles because he was the first author of walk books and is credited with being the inspiration of the Ramblers Association.

Headstone of 'Walker Miles'

4. The footpath continued past the end of the churchyard. We crossed two small footbridges, keeping the glebe pond on our left. Where the footpath emerged at a field, we turned right at the hedge line until it reached a service road with outbuildings on our right. After passing through two gates, we turned right, passing ponds on our left before turning right to a service road that led to the B2236 road. We turned right and noticed on our left an impressive timber-framed house, which would have accommodated the mill master and a little further on a milestone with directions to London. We continued along the B road, crossed Church Lane and on to The Enterdent. This was the site of an old quarry. At the side of White Cottage, we followed a

public footpath up Tilburstow Hill, with signs of the old quarry workings on our right. We ignored all side paths until we reached the top of the hill when we descended to Tilburstow Hill Road. We turned left in this road for a short distance until it crossed the Greensand Way. We crossed the road and followed the bridleway (part of the Greensand Way) at the side of Rabies Heath Wood with signs of earlier quarry workings. This BW ultimately emerged at a C road, where we turned up right to Rabies Heath Road.

Mill Master's house

5. At Snatt's Hill House on the corner, we crossed Rabies Heath Road to a public footpath, which led straight ahead through open fields to a copse (enclosing further quarry workings) on our left. This path eventually emerged at the service road of Garston Hall. We followed the service road down to Ivy Mill Lane. Here, we turned right and where the lane bent to the left, we took the footpath parallel to the lane and noticed the site of what would have been the watermill. At this stage we re-joined the lane, passed the village school on our right and reached the village green from where we had started our walk.

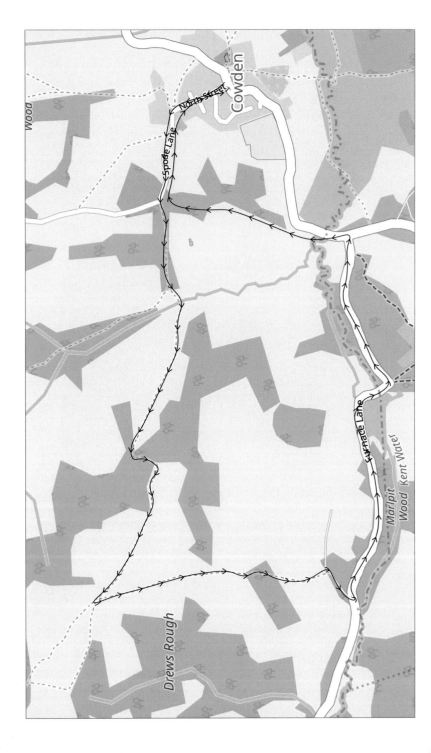

16. When Cowden Was the Hub of the Iron Industry

Circular Walk from Cowden Village

(5 Miles)

OS Explorer Map 147

Grid REF: TQ 466406

1. We started this walk from the Church of St Mary Magdalene in the centre of Cowden village. The village can be accessed by an occasional bus service on the Edenbridge/Tunbridge Wells route.

2. The Church is early medieval and is perhaps best known for its crooked spire, which can be seen to move in high winds or when the bells are rung. Since it has remained intact for nearly 700 years however, it is unlikely to fall any time soon. This off centre spire was, no doubt, the inspiration of the local rhyme

    "Cowden Church, crooked steeple
    Lying priest, deceitful people."

    This rhyme would probably have originated in Hartfield and referred to an inter-parish dispute, over which parish should bear the cost of arranging the funeral of a pauper. These sorts of disputes were commonplace at one time and it was not unknown for corpses to be dragged over a parish boundary so that another parish should bear the cost of the funeral.

3. From the church, we walked along the High Street in a Westerly direction until we met North Street on the right. Where this road bends left, it becomes Spode Lane, leading out of the village. We left the lane when it went right and walked straight ahead through the grounds of Waystrode Manor (FP658, part of the Sussex Border Path). We passed the early medieval

timber-framed manor house with a sunken roof. There are two other manor houses of similar vintage in the vicinity – Crippenden and Leighton.

4. At the end of the driveway we entered the woods by a gate and when we met the junction with FP661 leading to Leighton Manor, we turned left and crossed a narrow footbridge over a stream. Emerging from the woods, we crossed diagonally right over two fields and entered woodland, where the path turned left and then right. When we reached a gate, we passed into a field with a hedge. We walked slightly uphill to another gate and turned to see the spire of Cowden Church in the distance behind us.

5. We passed through the gate and ignoring FP657 on our left, which led to Pondtail in Furnace Lane, we walked diagonally right to a large open field. We aimed for a copse with an adjacent pond on the far side of the field, and walked past the left of the copse to a gate in the corner.

6. We passed through woodland to a clearing and a junction of paths. We ignored BW635 to Crippenden Manor to our right, and FP657 diagonally right to Dry Hill (the site of an Iron-Age Fort). We walked straight ahead through a small stretch of woodland to an open field, where we followed the hedge line to our right to a T-junction at BW654. We turned left and walked along the hedge line to a gate.

7. We passed through the gate, turned right and walked round two sides of the field. This BW becomes BW655, which led through woodland and descended to Hollow Lane.

8. We turned left in this road and soon passed Scarletts – a medieval timber-framed farmhouse which had fallen into a sad case of neglect, but it is now being restored. In medieval times, this was the site of a furnace for making iron. This road runs alongside Kent Water – a river that marks the county boundary between Kent and Sussex. As the road approaches Cowden, it

changes its name to Furnace Lane. We passed Pondtail Rough, another house being restored with a *Horsham Slab* roof to the front and a long cat slide roof at the back. Kent Water opens out into the old furnace ponds, which were the centre of the local Iron Industry, and the remains of a watermill. The road turned right and then left until a T-junction at Holtye Hill Road.

Waystrode Manor

9. There, we turned left and crossed Kitford Bridge. Some years ago there was speculation that oil might have been discovered but drilling proved negative. Just beyond the bridge, we entered a field on our left by FP665, where we proceeded at the side of a hedge on our right through two fields. This path then became enclosed with the garden of Waystrode Manor on our left. The path emerged at Spode Lane, where we had entered the Manor grounds at the beginning of the walk. We then retraced our steps via Spode Lane and North Street to the Church in the High Street.

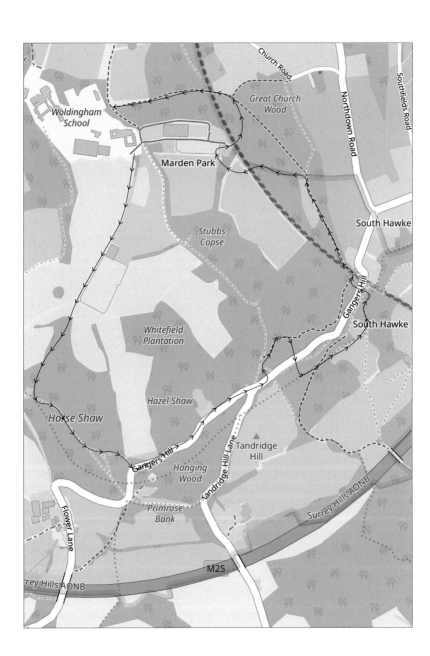

17. Before There Was a Woldingham Village

Circular Walk from Woldingham RT

(5 Miles)

OS Explorer Map 146

Grid REF: TQ 37354

1. We started this walk from the Woodland Trust's Marden Park car park at South Hawke Ganger's Lane on the north of M25 and south of Woldingham. The nearest railway station is Oxted and the nearest bus route would be the Hurst Green/Redhill Bus (410), which runs along the A25.

2. This land is owned and maintained by the Woodland Trust. From the car park, we followed the wide path through the Great Church Wood signposted to Woldingham Station. After walking about half a mile, we reached a waymark on our right, pointing to a set of 50 steps. This led into the Great Church Wood, a good spot to see bluebells in the spring. At the top of the steps, we turned left alongside the ridge until we came to a fork, where we turned right to a wooden gate out of the woods, with North Downs Golf Course on our right. We turned right out of the gate to Church Road so that we could make a slight diversion to see St Agatha's Church. This Church was originally built in the 13th century but was re-built in 1832 and restored in 1889. The Church probably owed its existence to Marden Park House, now the site of Woldingham Girls' School, but originally the site of the manor house.

3. We retraced our steps past the wooden gate, down an enclosed path to a footpath junction with a signpost pointing to Woldingham Station. It is interesting to note that this station was originally called Marden

Park because the railway line was constructed before the 20th-century village of Woldingham. We took the next turning on the right and noticed the tree trunks that would have been blown down in the 1987 hurricane. Our path turned right and took us over the edge of the railway tunnel to the other end of Church Road.

St Agatha's chapel

4. We turned left in Church Road and at the next signpost turned left over a railway bridge. Our path then turned sharp right and then sharp left to the Farm Road (public footpath) at Marden Park, with a view of Woldingham Village on the hillside. We now turned left, parallel to the railway line and parallel to a service road (public bridleway), which runs from Woldingham Station to Woldingham Girls' School. Our bridleway carried straight on, past some oil tanks to the school and a small cemetery for the local nuns. We turned right past the school and then left along a driveway (public driveway) to South Lodge – possibly a gatehouse to Marden Park House in earlier days.

Great Church Wood

5. At this point, we joined the North Downs Way. We turned left, up an enclosed footpath, into woodland, emerging into an open space with spectacular views to Godstone, Bletchingley and beyond to the Ashdown Forest. Our path then re-entered woodland and followed the North Downs Way to Tandridge Hill Lane, where our path ran next to the road until we reached Gangers Hill. Here, we walked along the road for a few yards and then took the public footpath on the right that ran parallel to the road. This path emerged at a viewing point with a display board showing all points south. After passing the viewing point, our path reached a set of steps to our left. These steps led back to the road at Gangers Hill and the Marden Park car park, from where we had started our walk.

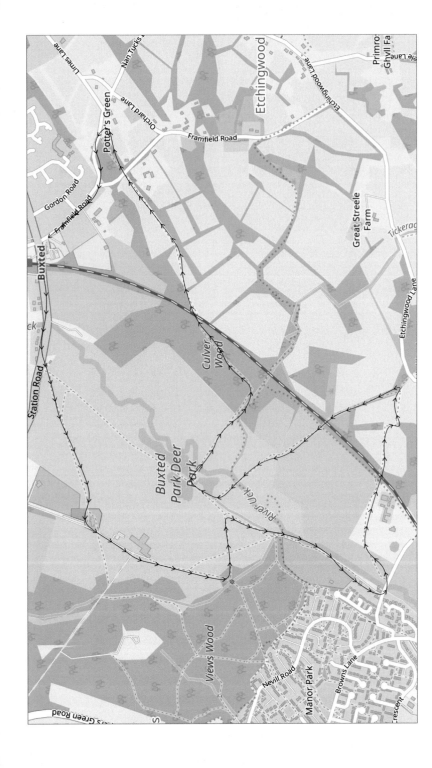

18. Through the Deer Park

Circular Walk from Buxted

(5 Miles)

OS Explorer Map 147

Grid REF: TQ 497233

1. This walk is best accessed by train on the London Bridge/East Croydon/Uckfield line or by the 248 Bus (Uckfield Hadlow Down) or 249 Bus (Uckfield Crowborough).

2. If you arrive by train and pass through the waiting room/ticket office, you may notice a table with an incomplete, large-sized jigsaw puzzle. There is a tradition that anyone passing this table should add a piece to this jigsaw puzzle before departing.

3. From the railway station, we turned right into Station Road (A272). After passing under a railway bridge and over a river bridge, we followed the main road until we saw the noticeboard for the Buxted Park Hotel on the opposite side of the road.

Buxted Manor House

4. Here we took a footpath, passed through a kissing gate and walked slightly uphill across open heathland. At a signpost, we took the right fork and made our way to St Margaret's Church. This Church is dedicated to Queen Margaret, the wife of King Malcolm of Scotland. (The story of his restoration to the throne after Macbeth's murder of his father, Duncan, is related in Shakespeare's tragedy.) The church was built in 1250 and originally encompassed several other parishes. In earlier days the village was located around the Church. In the early 19th century, however, the 3rd Earl of Liverpool had the whole village demolished and re-built in its present position in order that he could enlarge the deer park and afford himself greater seclusion. We noticed a fine avenue of lime trees from the church to the main road.

5. From the churchyard, we turned left along the driveway, past what is now a hotel but was earlier the site of the manor house. At the end of the driveway we entered a field by a small gate and turned left. This path is a part of the Weald Way long distance path. This path led on until we reached a copse, where we descended to a footbridge over a stream. Instead of crossing the footbridge, we took the path out of the copse through a gate and walked in a straight line to the right of a fence. When this path reached a kissing gate, we turned sharp right, entered a copse, passed through a kissing gate and crossed a footbridge until we reached the bank of the River Uck. Here, we turned right with the river on our left and a rugby ground on our right. We followed the riverside path until we reached the hamlet of Hempstead.

6. At the service road, we turned left and noticed what was once an impressive watermill. Past the watermill, we turned left along a footpath, across a stile on our right and diagonally across two fields, where animals from a charitable sanctuary were grazing, and down a flight of steps to the Buxted/Uckfield Railway Line. We walked up another flight of steps and crossed two fields until we reached a junction with another footpath. We

turned left on this path and followed it until it crossed the railway line a second time by another two flights of steps. In this field, we walked diagonally right to the corner. At one time, it was necessary to climb a ladder stile, known locally as the devil's ladder, in order to exit this field. We passed through a deer gate, and soon saw the back of the hotel on our left. Our path crossed two footbridges and emerged at a signpost, where we turned right and followed the path out of the Deer Park by a deer gate.

Hempstead watermill

7. Our path led into Culver Wood at the side of a stream. Our path led out of the woods and on to a subway under the railway line. In the field on the opposite side of the railway line, we walked diagonally left to a squeeze stile, and followed the footpath to a C road at Mascall's Farm. We crossed the road and followed the footpath through the woodland to Limes Lane. Here, we turned left until the lane joined Framfield Road, leading back to the A272 road and Buxted Station.

19. When Estates Had Their Own Firecrews

Linear Walk from Dorking to Wotton Hatch

(5 Miles)

OS Explorer Map 146

Grid REF: TQ 171502

1. This walk is best accessed by train to Dorking Deep-dene (on the Guildford-Redhill line), or Dorking North (on the line from London Waterloo). Also there are several local bus routes.

2. From either station we crossed the dual carriageway (A24), turned left and took the first turning on our right (London Road). We passed the remains of Pass-brook Mill (C 1650) and took the public footpath on our right, at Tutts Close. This enclosed path led to Meadow Bank Park, through which Pipps Brook ran. We noticed at this entrance to the park what would have been the mill pond for Passbrook Mill. We crossed the park to the far end where fences enclosed the Dorking Club football ground, and reached Chalk Pit Lane. We crossed this road, passed a parade of shops and turned right up Ranmore Road. We continued along this road, ignoring Station Road to our left, which would have led to Dorking West Station, and we crossed a railway bridge and school before taking a footpath on our left. This path led through a copse, which ran parallel to the railway line and the school playing fields.

3. On emerging from the copse, we left the main path to take a NT marked path on our left, to walk diago-nally across a field to a hedge at the side of the railway line. We turned right, at the side of the hedge, and walked through two fields to a level-crossing. Here, we

crossed the railway line and followed the footpath to Clay Copse. We ignored the path to our left and walked through the copse. When our path emerged at the other end of the copse, we walked along the side of two fields, crossed a footbridge over Pipps Brook and followed the driveway up to the A25 at Milton Street.

Fire station

4. We crossed the A25 into Milton Street and noticed the fire station of yesteryear at Old Bury Hill Gardens. Walking through Milton Street, we admired the varied architectural styles of the different houses. On the right hand side of the street, little footbridges over a stream connected the houses to the road. We turned right, over one of these bridges, with a waymark that indicated we had now joined the Greensand Way. Our path followed fences at the back of houses and following the waymarks, it turned right to a common and the churchyard of Westcott Church – one of many designed by Sir Gilbert Scott. Our path – still part of the Greensand Way – led back to the A25 at Rookery Drive (perhaps, a former gatehouse to an estate).

House and waterfall, Westcott

5. We walked along Railway Drive, admired a water feature in one of the gardens we passed through, and at a house called Cedars, we turned left along a footpath. At a path junction by a stile, we turned right, uphill on the Greensand Way Path through Sylvanus Wood to a byway opposite. This led to the public road at Sheep House Lane. Here we turned right, taking the footpath parallel to the lane and over the access road to a business park until we reached the A25 again – this time at the Wotton Hatch pub. Once upon a time, it was an ale house for local farmworkers but now a thriving pub/restaurant, attracting punters who drive out from Dorking and Guildford. Opposite the pub, we were able to catch a bus back to Dorking.

20. A Picturesque Moated Manor House off the Beaten Track

Walk from Shipbourne Common to Underriver and Return

(5 Miles)

Grid REF: TQ 594522

1. There is a car park on the common road at Shipbourne Village and several other parking spaces in the vicinity. The village can also be accessed by bus no. 222 (Tunbridge Wells/Wrotham) and 404 from Sevenoaks.

2. We crossed the A227 road opposite the Chaser PH, and walked through the churchyard of St Giles Church, re-built in 1722. At the back of the churchyard is a junction of three paths. We took the footpath marked as 'Greensand Way' diagonally right. We followed this path with fencing on our right, until we reached a cross track. We continued in the same direction with a copse on our left, until our path entered South Seers Wood. Emerging from the other end of the woods, we crossed two grazing fields to Mote Road. Here, we turned right and followed the road to Ightham Mote.

Ightham Mote

3. Ightham Mote is a 14th century moated manor house – heavily timber-framed and built of Kentish rag stone. At one time it had fallen into neglect, but in recent years has painstakingly been restored by the National Trust. The banqueting hall and chapel are two of the most outstanding features.

Ightham Mote

4. Leaving Ightham Mote behind, we turned sharp left through the farmyard of Mote Farm. Our bridleway (still part of the Greensand Way) continued under the brow of Wilmot Hill and Shingle Hill with stunning views to the south towards the Ashdown Forest and beyond to the South Downs. On our way, we ignored side paths to the right and left, and noticed the brick-encased well outside Wilmot Cottage. We followed the Greensand Way Path through Shingle Hill Wood to a tarmac by-way, where we turned left down a steep hill to a C road at Absolam's Farm. We turned right in this road, which led us after half a mile to crossroads at Underriver Village.

5. Here, we turned left and just before 'The Forge' (an imposing house on our left), we turned left at a stile (FP153), and then followed a straight line through

five fields with a fine view in the last field of Under-river House – an impressive building with Georgian windows. Where our path emerged at a B road in front of Underriver House, we turned left for a few yards and then right along a service road (public footpath) past Underriver House Cottages and Boundary Farm to the back of Underriver House. Our path then led through a copse and into a field with woodland to our left. We followed this path to a farmyard and then followed a straight line across three more fields to a copse at Budds Green, Mote Road.

6. We turned left in this road for a few yards, and then right on FP MR 396 through Cold Blows Wood. We ignored side paths through the woods until we reached a T-junction where we turned right. This path took us out of the woods into arable fields with views of Ship-bourne Church in front of us. We then followed the path in a straight line to the churchyard of St Giles Church, and the A227 road with the Chaser Inn on our right. We crossed the road to return to the car park at Shipbourne Common.

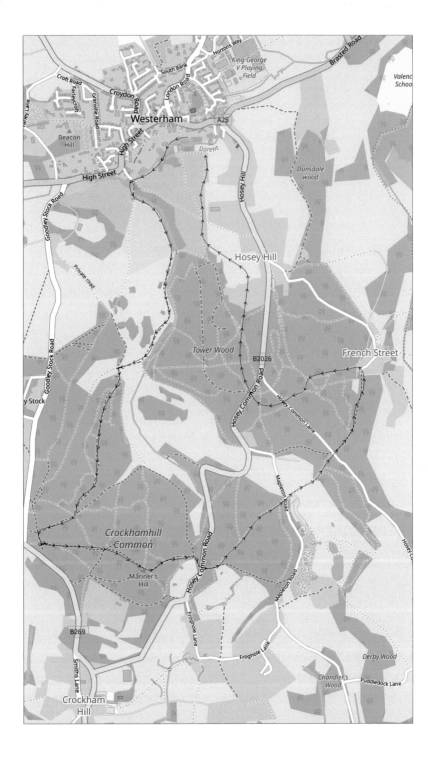

21. To See Churchill's House

Circular Walk from Hosey Common

(6 miles)

OS Explorer Mar 147

Grid REF: TQ 453531

1. The start of the walk is best accessed by car. There is an occasional bus service between East Grinstead and Westerham. Otherwise, the starting point is approximately one mile up the Hosey Hill, from Westerham on the bus route between Redhill and Sevenoaks.

Westerham village green

2. From the car park outside the old school house, we crossed Hosey Hill (B2026 road) and entered the woods at the side of Charts Edge (a private garden with an array of unusual plants open to the public during the summer) on FP380. Where the path reached a T-junction with FP352, we turned right down FP352 at the back of Charts Edge. Where the path emerged out of the woods, at a kissing gate, we turned right up a

hill and down the other side, with views of Westerham and the North Downs beyond. This led to the banks of the River Darenth, which rises on Crockham Hill Common, although at certain times of the year, the view of the river can be obscured by undergrowth. We turned left to a kissing gate along FP348 until we came to Mill Lane opposite the lake at Squerryes (A stately house built in 1681 and inhabited by the Warde family since 1731). We turned left in Mill Lane, past the ruins of the watermill on the left, which obviously gave its name to the lane. At a lodge house where the path divides, we walked uphill on FP353. At the top of the hill by a kissing gate we looked back again at the view of the town and church in the valley and the North Downs beyond. We continued on this path through the woods (ignoring the cross path FP349 at the edge of the woods) until we reached another lodge house, where we took the second path on our left (FP359) just short of Goodley Stock Road. (This path is part of the Greensand Way long distance path.) We followed this path, ignoring side paths until a clearing by a service road, where are situated the Red House, Octavias Hill's home and the cottage inhabited by her gardener. All three gardens are open to the public occasionally, under the National Gardens Scheme, and enjoy spectacular views across the Eden Valley and beyond to the Ashdown Forest.

3. We took the tarmac driveway diagonally left on FP366, passed a cottage on our right, The Warren, and dropped down through the woods – ignoring the side paths to the left and right – to Hosey Common Road. On the right hand side, just before the road, is the site where a WW2 children's home accommodating youngsters evacuated from the London Blitz was bombed by a stray enemy aircraft returning to Germany. The mass grave with a headstone recounting the event is located in the cemetery by Edenbridge Parish Church Crossing Hosey Common Road. We climbed Mariner's Hill, opposite on FP365 and at the top, we turned sharp left and followed the path through the woods until it

dropped down to Mapleton Road by the entrance to Chartwell, the National Trust Property and former home of Winston Churchill, who transformed a derelict farmhouse into the grand house we see today. We climbed the hill at the side of Chartwell grounds on FP375 crossing Hosey Common Lane to the edge of the hamlet of French St where we turned left to a service road (FP382), which passed a house on the left and then through the woods to Hosey Common Lane. At a cross-path in the woods, we walked straight on. Where the paths forked, we took the right hand fork. At Hosey Common Lane, we turned right past the Evergreen Acres Farm on our left, and then took FP384 on our left to Hosey Common Road and the edge of the Squerryes Estate. After crossing the road, we took the diagonal path on our right (FP352), through more woods at the edge of the estate until a path on our right which passed by the side of Charts Edge on our left, back to Hosey Common Road and the car park at the old school house.